Countries of the World

Mexico

by Michael Dahl

Bridgestone Books
an Imprint of Capstone Press

Bridgestone Books are published by Capstone Press
818 North Willow Street, Mankato, Minnesota 56001
Copyright © 1997 by Capstone Press
All rights reserved
Printed in the United States of America

Library of Congress Cataloging-in-Publication Data
Dahl, Michael.
    Mexico/by Michael Dahl.
    p. cm.--(Countries of the world)
    Includes bibliographical references and index.
    Summary: Discusses the history, landscape, people, and culture of Mexico.
    ISBN 1-56065-476-7
    1. Mexico--Juvenile literature. [1. Mexico.] I. Title.
II. Series: Countries of the world (Mankato, Minn.)
F1208.5D34   1997
972--DC21

96-50160
CIP
AC

Bridgestone Books would like to thank the Mexican Cultural Institute for their help with this project.

Photo credits
Flag Research Center, 4
FPG/Myers, 5; Reiff, 7; Murphy, 13; Scocozza, 15; Foster, 17; Gridley, 21
Unicorn, 9, 11, 19

Table of Contents

Fast Facts

Name: Mexico

Capital: Mexico City

Population: More than 92 million people

Language: Spanish

Religion: Mostly Roman Catholic

Size: 756,066 square miles (1,965,772 square kilometers) *Mexico is four times larger than the U.S. state of Texas.*

Crops: coffee, cotton, and wheat

Maps

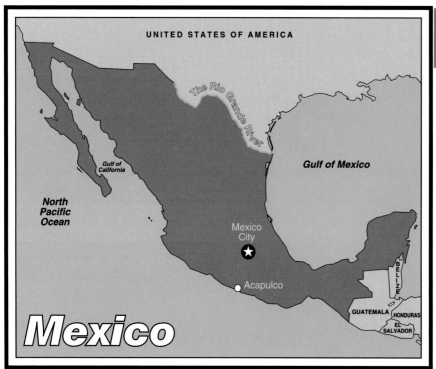

Flag

Mexico's flag is made of three up-and-down stripes. The left stripe is green. It stands for hope. The middle is white. It stands for purity. The right stripe is red. It stands for the blood of Mexican people. Many died fighting for freedom.

There is a drawing in the white stripe. It is of an eagle on a cactus tree. The eagle is eating a snake. The picture is based on an Aztec legend. Aztecs are Indian people. They lived in Mexico before Spanish people. Spanish people came to Mexico from Spain.

Currency

Mexican currency is the peso. One peso equals 100 centavos.

It takes seven pesos to equal one U.S. dollar.

Land of Mexico

Mexico is part of Latin America. It is also the southern neighbor of the United States. It is four times larger than the U.S. state of Texas.

Mexico is shaped like a fat fish hook. Inside the hook lies the Gulf of Mexico. The Pacific Ocean borders Mexico's west coast. Many people visit Mexico to relax on its beaches.

Mexico is home to many different types of land. Two mountain ranges cut through Mexico. Some parts of Mexico are covered by deserts. Tropical jungles cover other areas.

Mountains and jungles cover most of Mexico.

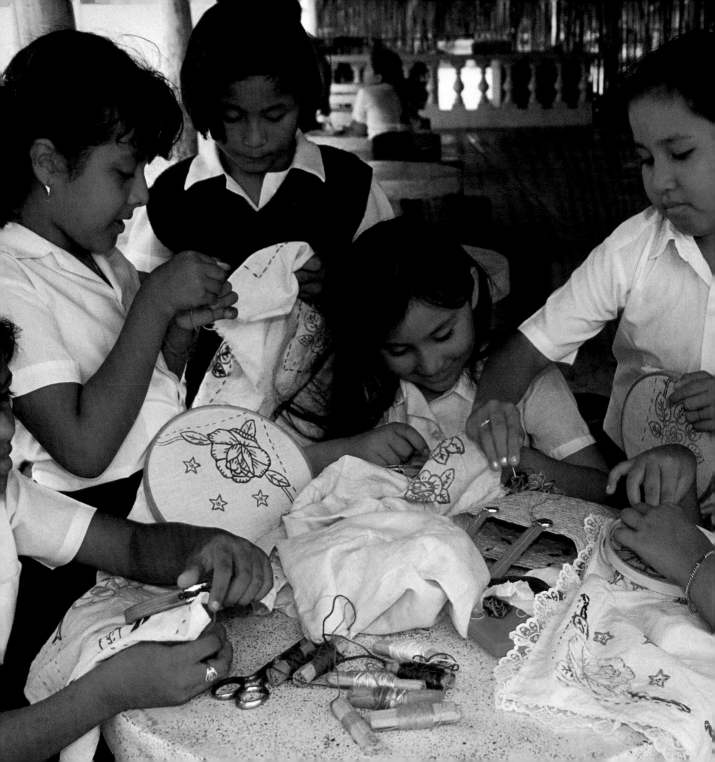

Going to School

Mexico's government provides free education for children. These are the public schools. Mexico also has private schools.

Schools in large cities are a lot like North American schools. Students learn art, sports, and other activities. Only most Mexican students must wear a uniform.

Schools in small towns do not have much money. The school building is used for things like government meetings, too.

Mexico's original people were Mayan or Aztec Indians. People whose families were originally Aztec or Mayan are called Mexican-Indians. Often they speak different languages. Some of them learn how to speak Spanish only in school.

Children make many things in art class.

At Home

Most Mexicans live in cities. Many live in apartment buildings. Others live in houses. In the middle of most Spanish-style houses is a patio. Most children's games and activities take place on the patio.

Poor people live in shacks. Petates (pay-TAH-tays) are straw mats used for beds. Their dishes are made of clay.

Country houses are made of stone or adobe. Adobe is dried mud. This keeps the houses cool during the day. Roofs are made of palm tree leaves.

Some houses are made out of rock. This rock comes from the volcanoes found in Mexico. Volcanoes are holes in the crust of the earth. They can erupt, or blow up.

Country houses have roofs made of palm tree leaves.

Clothes

Most Mexican clothes are like clothes worn in the United States and Canada. But some things are different.

Mexican ranchers wear hats called sombreros (som-BRER-ohs). This protects them from Mexico's hot sun. Leather pants called chaps protect their legs from cactus plants.

Ponchos (PON-chohs) protect people from the rain. Serapes (sah-RAH-pehs) are colorful blankets that keep people warm.

Sometimes Mexican-Indian people dress up to perform traditional dances. Some women wear an outfit called china poblana (CHEE-nah poh-BLAH-nah). This is a full skirt and a short-sleeved, decorated blouse. They tie a colored sash around their waist. Women dance the Mexican hat dance wearing china poblana.

Women dance while wearing china poblana.

Tortillas and Mole

People around the world enjoy Mexican food. Mexico introduced corn, chocolate, and chilies to the world. Corn is still an important food in Mexico.

Corn is used to make tortillas. These are like thin pancakes. Mexicans fill them with meat, cheese, and vegetables. Fried beans are served with many meals.

Mexicans even drink corn. Corn is made into a drink called atole (ah-TOH-leh). Mexicans drink it often for breakfast. It is thick like a milkshake.

Sometimes Mexicans cover meat with a special sauce called mole (moh-LAY). Mole is made of spices and chocolate.

Meat, cheese, and vegetables fill tortillas.

Animals of Mexico

Lizards and coyotes roam Mexico's northern deserts. A rare rabbit lives in Mexico. It is called the volcano rabbit. It can only be seen near Mexican volcanoes.

Jaguars live in Mexico's southern jungles. The jaguar is the largest wild cat in North America. Its yellow fur is covered with black spots. At night, jaguars hunt for deer or turtles to eat.

The chihuahua (chee-WAH-wah) is the world's smallest dog. It comes from Mexico. The tiny dog is named for a Mexican state.

Visitors can see gray whales in the water off of Mexico's western coast. Every winter the whales return to the warm waters near Mexico. There they have their young, called calves.

Lizards roam Mexico's northern deserts.

Bullfights, Futbol, and Charreria

Bullfighting has many fans in Mexico. Matadors (ma-TA-dor-ehs) fight bulls. They try to kill a wild bull with a sword.

Matadors wear bright costumes called suits of light. Matadors tire bulls by teasing them with red capes. Then the matador fights the bull with a sword.

Mexican people also enjoy futbol (FOOT-bohl). Futbol is also known as soccer. The Azteca Stadium in Mexico City holds 100,000 futbol fans.

Charreria (char-RER-ee-ah) is another Mexican sport. It is a lot like a rodeo. Charros (CHAR-ros) are cowboys who compete in the events. One event is especially dangerous. A charro tries to roll a bull onto its back. The charro does this by using the bull's tail.

Matadors tire wild bulls by teasing them with capes.

The World's Largest City

Mexico City is the capital of Mexico. It is the largest city in the world. Ten million people live in Mexico City. It is also the highest city in North America.

A quarter of Mexico's factories are in Mexico City. People move there to work. Some factories make automobile parts and motors. Others make clothes and products out of steel.

Mexico City is the oldest city in North America. Long ago, the Aztec people lived there. Many of their buildings and pyramids are still standing. Visitors come from around the world to see them.

People from around the world visit Aztec pyramids.

Hands On: Run a Mexican Race

The Tarahumara (tah-rah-hoo-MAH-rah) Indians are famous for their running abilities. Men, women, and children run long distances each day.

Follow these rules to run a Tarahumara race.

1. You must race in groups. The groups are made up of three or more runners.
2. Each group is given a small ball.
3. When the groups run, they kick the ball. The groups work together. Runners pass the ball between them.
4. Choose a goal or finish line. The first group to reach the goal wins.
5. Remember, groups must reach the goal together with their ball.

The Tarahumara run races of 100 miles (160 kilometers). Their races can last up to three days. They celebrate the end of the race with a party.

Learn to Speak Spanish

boy	nino	(NEEN-yoh)
food	comida	(koh-MEE-dah)
girl	nina	(NEEN-yah)
good morning	buenos dias	(bway-nohs DEE-ahs)
good bye	adios	(ah-dee-OHS)
hello	hola	(OH-lah)
house	casa	(KAH-sah)
thank you	gracias	(GRAH-see-us)

Words to Know

adobe (ah-DOH-bee)—blocks made of dried mud

atole (ah-TOH-leh)—a drink made from corn

Aztec (AZ-tek)—Indian people who lived in Mexico before Spanish people settled there

chihuahua (chee-WAH-wah)—the world's smallest dog; came from Mexico

matador (ma-TA-dor)—a bullfighter

mole (moh-LAY)—a sauce made of spices and chocolate

petate (pay-TAH-tay)—a straw mat used for a bed

serape (sah-RAH-peh)—a colorful blanket

siesta (see-EHS-tah)—a long afternoon nap

sombrero (sohm-BRER-oh)—a wide-brimmed hat

tortilla (tor-TEE-yahs)—a thin corn pancake

Read More

Braun, Barbara. *A Weekend with Diego Rivera*. New York: Rizzoli, 1994.
Bulmer-Thomas, Barbara. *Journey Through Mexico*. New York: Troll
    Associates, 1991.
Coronado, Rose. *Cooking the Mexican Way*. Minneapolis: Lerner, 1982.
Jacobsen, Karen. *Mexico*. Chicago: Children's Press, 1982.

Useful Addresses and Internet Sites

Embassy of Mexico
1911 Pennsylvania Avenue NW
Washington, DC 20006

Mexican Cultural Institute
2829 16th Street NW
Washington, DC 20009

Mexican Embassy in Canada
http://www.DocuWeb.ca/Mexico/1-engl/main96.html

Mexican Consulate in New York
http://quickLink.com/Mexico

Index